First World War
and Army of Occupation
War Diary
France, Belgium and Germany

57 DIVISION
170 Infantry Brigade
King's Own (Royal Lancaster Regiment)
2/5th Battalion
6 February 1917 - 31 March 1918

WO95/2979/7

The Naval & Military Press Ltd
www.nmarchive.com
Published in association with The National Archives

Published by

The Naval & Military Press Ltd

Unit 10 Ridgewood Industrial Park,

Uckfield, East Sussex,

TN22 5QE England

Tel: +44 (0) 1825 749494

www.naval-military-press.com

www.nmarchive.com

This diary has been reprinted in facsimile from the original. Any imperfections are inevitably reproduced and the quality may fall short of modern type and cartographic standards.

© **Crown Copyright**
Images reproduced by permission of The National Archives, London, England, 2015.

Contents

Document type	Place/Title	Date From	Date To
Heading	WO95/2979-7		
Heading	War Diary Of 2/5th Bn The King's Own Royal Lancaster Regiment From 6th February 1917 To 28th February 1917		
War Diary	Southampton	06/02/1917	06/02/1917
War Diary	Le Havre	07/02/1917	08/02/1917
War Diary	Bailleul	10/02/1917	10/02/1917
War Diary	Outtersteene	11/02/1917	13/02/1917
War Diary	Sailly	13/02/1917	14/02/1917
War Diary	Cordonnerie Sector	15/02/1917	15/02/1917
War Diary	Sailly	16/02/1917	26/02/1917
Miscellaneous	The O.C. 2/5th Bn The King's Own R.L.R.	07/04/1917	07/04/1917
War Diary	Cordonnerie Trench	02/03/1917	09/03/1917
War Diary	Fleurbaix	15/03/1917	15/03/1917
War Diary	Boutillerie	17/03/1917	23/03/1917
War Diary	Fleurbaix	24/03/1917	31/03/1917
Miscellaneous	D.A.G. General H.Q. 3rd Echelon	01/05/1917	01/05/1917
War Diary	Boutillerie Sector	04/04/1917	04/04/1917
War Diary	Fleurbaix	04/04/1917	24/04/1917
War Diary	Boutillerie Sector	02/05/1917	10/05/1917
War Diary	Fleurbaix	12/05/1917	12/05/1917
War Diary	Boutillerie Sector	17/05/1917	25/05/1917
War Diary	Boutillerie Trench Sector	02/06/1917	02/07/1917
War Diary	Fleurbaix	02/07/1917	31/07/1917
Miscellaneous	Headquarters 170th Infantry Brigade	01/09/1917	01/09/1917
War Diary	Houplines Trench Sector	01/08/1917	01/08/1917
War Diary	Armentieres	01/08/1917	01/09/1917
War Diary	Houplines Trench Sector	03/09/1917	05/09/1917
War Diary	Armentieres	05/09/1917	06/09/1917
War Diary	Houplines Trench Sector	09/09/1917	09/09/1917
War Diary	Houplines Sector	10/09/1917	11/09/1917
War Diary	Armentieres	16/09/1917	16/09/1917
War Diary	De. Seule Camp Nieppe	18/09/1917	18/09/1917
War Diary	Ch. Bovelle	18/09/1917	18/09/1917
War Diary	L'Ecleme Near Lillers	19/09/1917	19/09/1917
War Diary	Auchy-Au-Bois	20/09/1917	24/09/1917
Miscellaneous	Headquarters 170th. Infantry Brigade	01/11/1917	01/11/1917
War Diary	Auchy Au Bois	01/10/1917	06/10/1917
War Diary	Enguinegate	07/10/1917	07/10/1917
War Diary	Auchy Au Bois	17/10/1917	17/10/1917
War Diary	Coin Perdu	18/10/1917	18/10/1917
War Diary	Penton Camp Proven Belgium	22/10/1917	22/10/1917
War Diary	Penton Camp	23/10/1917	23/10/1917
War Diary	Wolf Camp Elverdinghe	24/10/1917	24/10/1917
War Diary	Eagle Trench Schreiboom nr Poelcappelle	25/10/1917	25/10/1917
War Diary	Shaap Balie	26/10/1917	26/10/1917
War Diary	Pitchcott Camp Proven Area No1	27/10/1917	27/10/1917
War Diary	Pitchcott Camp Proven Belgium	28/10/1917	28/10/1917
War Diary	Pitchcott Camp Proven	29/10/1917	30/10/1917
Miscellaneous	Headquarters 170th Infantry Brigade	01/12/1917	01/12/1917

War Diary	Proven Belgium	04/11/1917	04/11/1917
War Diary	Pitchcott Camp Proven	08/11/1917	08/11/1917
War Diary	Sanghem France	09/11/1917	09/11/1917
War Diary	Sanghem Licques	11/11/1917	11/11/1917
War Diary	Sanghem	14/11/1917	30/11/1917
War Diary	Sanghem France Map Ref Calais 131/100000	01/12/1917	01/12/1917
War Diary	Guemy France Map Ref Harebrouck	07/12/1917	07/12/1917
War Diary	Sanghem France	09/12/1917	09/12/1917
War Diary	Proven	12/12/1917	12/12/1917
War Diary	Bapaume Camp	15/12/1917	16/12/1917
War Diary	H.Camp (A.10.a.0.2)	17/12/1917	17/12/1917
War Diary	H.Camp	18/12/1917	30/12/1917
War Diary	Petworth Camp (Sheet 19 X.25.d.4.7	31/12/1917	31/12/1917
Heading	War Diary 2/5th Bn. The King's Own (Royal Lancaster) Regt. January 1918		
War Diary	Petworth Camp	01/01/1918	02/01/1918
War Diary	Waterlands Camp	03/01/1918	03/01/1918
War Diary	Chapelle Sector	08/01/1918	08/01/1918
War Diary	Chapelle Sector (Renames Nez Macquart)	09/01/1918	09/01/1918
War Diary	Erquinghem	15/01/1918	29/01/1918
War Diary	Honours & Awards	17/01/1918	21/01/1918
War Diary	Casualties	01/01/1918	24/01/1918
Heading	War Diary 2/5 Batt The Kings Own R. Lanc. Regt February 1918		
War Diary	Erquinghem (H.4.d.1.4)	01/02/1918	01/02/1918
War Diary	Hollebecque Camp (B.19.b.8.7)	05/02/1918	07/02/1918
War Diary	Wez Macquart Section (I.14.d.4.8)	09/02/1918	11/02/1918
War Diary	Estaires L,30,b,2.9	13/02/1918	13/02/1918
War Diary	St Hilaire T 5d 5.8	14/02/1918	27/02/1918
Miscellaneous	Headquarters 170th Infantry Brigade	31/03/1918	31/03/1918
War Diary	St. Hilaire	01/03/1918	01/03/1918
War Diary	Le Sart	02/03/1918	02/03/1918
War Diary	Estaires	10/03/1918	10/03/1918
War Diary	Merville	16/03/1918	16/03/1918
War Diary	Neuf Berquin	19/03/1918	19/03/1918
War Diary	Bois Grenier	20/03/1918	27/03/1918
War Diary	Nouveau Monde	27/03/1918	29/03/1918
War Diary	S Of Chapelle D'Armentieres	30/03/1918	31/03/1918

wasn't 20/9 (1) 9:50am

wasn't 20/9 (1) 9:50am

CONFIDENTIAL

WAR DIARY

of

2/5th Bn. The King's Own Royal Lancaster Regiment.

from 6th February, 1917. to 28th February 1917.

Army Form C. 2118

WAR DIARY
or
INTELLIGENCE SUMMARY
(Erase heading not required.)

2/5 & 7th The King's Own Royal Lancaster Regt.

Instructions regarding War Diaries and Intelligence Summaries are contained in F.S. Regs., Part II. and the Staff Manual respectively. Title Pages will be prepared in manuscript.

Place	Date	Hour	Summary of Events and Information	Remarks and references to Appendices
SOUTHAMPTON	6/2/17	16:15	16 Officers 570 O.R. sailed from SOUTHAMPTON on "S.S. Queen Alexandra" arriving	7A/
do	do	21:0	LE HAVRE at 23 o'clock. Crossing very rough. 10 Officers 381 O.R. sailed from SOUTHAMPTON in "S.S. Manchester Importer" arriving	
LE HAVRE	7/2/17	11:0	LE HAVRE 11 o'clock the following day (7/2/17)	7A/
do	7/2/17	7:0	The first party disembarked and marched to No 1 Rest Camp	7A/
do	7/2/17	11:30	Second party disembarked and marched to No 1 Rest Camp	7A/
do	do	23:0	Received orders for entrainment to commence on following day.	7A/
do	8/2/17	8:0	1st Party of 50 entrained	7A/
do	do	12:0	2nd Party of 100 entrained	7A/
do	do	17:0	3rd Party of 50 entrained	7A/
do	do	20:30	Remainder of Battalion entrained	7A/
BAILLEUL	10/2/17	11:15	Detrained and proceeded to OUTTERSTEENE by march route. After the Bn was billeted, during the train journey of 39 hours only two halts were made, at MONTRELIER - BUCHY and ABBEVILLE. The accommodation at the latter place was extremely bad, only 75% of the troops being able to obtain hot drinks.	7A/
OUTTERSTEENE	11/2/17		Resting in Billets	7A/
do	12/2/17		Small Box Respirators issued to all Ranks.	7A/
do	12/2/17	20:0	Orders received for move to SAILLY	7A/
do	13/2/17	11:0	Left by march route for SAILLY	7A/
SAILLY	13/2/17	15:40	Troops billeted in SAILLY	7A/
do	14/2/17		Orders received to relieve the 2 R. W. Z. R. B. in the CORDONNERIE Trench Sector, at the rate of one Company per diem commencing on the 15/2/17	7A/

WAR DIARY
or
INTELLIGENCE SUMMARY

(Erase heading not required.) 2/5th The King's Own R.L. Regt

Army Form C. 2118

Place	Date	Hour	Summary of Events and Information	Remarks and references to Appendices
CORDONNERIE SECTOR. SAILLY	15/5/17	9.0	"A" Company relieved the centre company of the 2nd Bn. New Zealand Rifle Bde	7th
do.	16/5/17	9.0	"D" Company relieved the Coy of 2 Bn. N.Z.R.B. on left of sector. One O.Rs wounded	7th
do.	17/5/17	9.0	"C" Company relieved the Coy of 2 Bn N.Z.R.B. on right of Sector. Casualties two O.Rs wounded	7th
do.		14:0	Battalion H.Q. relieved B.H.Q. 2 Bn N.Z.R.B	7th
do.	18/5/17	7:25	"B" Coy relieved the fourth Coy of 2 Bn. N.Z.R.B. This completed the relief.	7th
do.	19/5/17		Casualties 2 O.R. killed	7th
do.	21/5/17		do 3 O.R. killed 7 wounded 1 Died of wounds	7th
do.	22/5/17	11:0	"A" Coy relieved by "D" Coy 2/5 Loyal North Lancashire Regt.	7th
do.	23/5/17	10:45	"D" Coy " " "C" Coy do do	7th
do.	24/5/17	10.5	"C" Coy " " A Coy do do	7th
do.	24/5/17	10.45	Batt. Headquarters relieved by B.H.Q. do do	7th
do.	25/5/17	11:30	"B" Coy relieved by "B" Coy 2/5 L.N.L.Regt. This completed the relief.	7th
SAILLY	26/5/17		The Battalion in Rest Billets (D Batt Divisional Reserve)	7th

Nuttage Lt Colonel
THE KINGS OWN R. LANCASTER REGT

A/~~283~~ 293

SUBJECT:- War Diary

From The O.C. 2/5th Bn The King's Own R.L.R.
      In the Field.

To   D.A.G.,
      General Headquarters,
      3rd Echelon.

      In accordance with G.R.O.1598, I forward herewith War Diary of this unit for the month of March, 1917, for your information.

                                      F.B.Seward Major,
                                              Commanding,
7/4/17.   2/5th Bn The King's Own R.L.R.

Army Form C. 2118

WAR DIARY or INTELLIGENCE SUMMARY

2/5 The King's Own R. Lanc. Regt.

March, 1917

(Erase heading not required.)

Instructions regarding War Diaries and Intelligence Summaries are contained in F.S. Regs., Part II. and the Staff Manual respectively. Title Pages will be prepared in manuscript.

Place	Date	Hour	Summary of Events and Information	Remarks and references to Appendices
CORDONNERIE TRENCH	2/3/17	16??	Took over left SECTOR of CORDONNERIE TRENCH relieving 2/5 Loyal North Lancashire Regt.	707
do	8/3/17		Casualties 3 O.Rs wounded	707
do	9/3/17	10.30	Relieved from CORDONNERIE by 2/4 Bn Loyal North Lanc. Regt. This Bn. going into billets in FLEURBAIX	707
FLEURBAIX	15/3/17	21:30	Relieved 4/5 Royal North Lanc Regt in BOUTILLERIE SECTOR	707
BOUTILLERIE	17/3/17		Casualties 1 O.R. wounded	707
do	18/3/17		Casualties Killed 1 O.R.	707
do	19/3/17		Casualties Wounded 2/Lieut E.L. WHALLEY and 1 O.R.	707
do	20/3/17		Casualties Killed 1 O.R. Wounded 4 O.Rs.	707
do	21/3/17		Casualties Wounded 2 O.R.	707
do	22/3/17	21.40	Enemy patrol of 9 men entered our trench but were immediately driven off leaving two rifles (numbers on No 7 Bn Business List). Our wounded 1 O.R.	707
do	23/3/17	20.30	Relieved by 4/5 Bn Loyal North Lanc. Regt. Bn going into billets in FLEURBAIX	707
FLEURBAIX	24/3/17	23	Summer Time came into force (one hour advance 23 & 24 meeting)	707
do	28/3/17	12.25	Bombardment of FLEURBAIX. Casualties Killed 8 O.Rs Wounded 2/Lt W.R. SLEIGH and 18 O.Rs	707
do	28/3/17	14.0	Accident at Brigade Bomb School. Casualties wounded Lt G.H. HUTCHINGSON, 2nd Lt W.S. WEBSTER (since died of wounds) E.T. FORGE; R. HALL; and 2 O.Rs.	707
do	29/3/17		Reinforcements 51 Os & 62 O.Rs	707
do	31/3/17	22:50	Relieved 4/5 Bn Loyal North Lanc Regt in BOUTILLERIE SECTOR.	707

F.D. Leveson Maj.
2/5th The King's Own R.L.Rgt

CONFIDENTIAL.

D.A.G.,
    General H.Q.,   3rd Echelon.

        In accordance with G.R.O 1508, I beg to forward herewith War Diary of the unit under my command for the month of April, 1917, for your information.

In the Field.
1/5/17

                      Lt.Colonel,
                      Commanding,
          2/5th Bn The King's Own R.L.R.

WAR DIARY or INTELLIGENCE SUMMARY

Army Form C. 2118.

2/5th Bn The King's Own Royal Lancaster Regt.

April 1917

(Erase heading not required.)

Instructions regarding War Diaries and Intelligence Summaries are contained in F.S. Regs., Part II. and the Staff Manual respectively. Title pages will be prepared in manuscript.

Hour, Date, Place	Summary of Events and Information	Remarks and references to Appendices
BOUTILLERIE SECTOR FLEURBAIX 4/4/17		
do 6/4/17	Casualties, 2nd Lt. I. GILLESPIE and two O.Rs wounded	
do 7/4/17	Casualties, Wounded one O.R.	
do 8/4/17	Casualties, Wounded one O.R.	
	Lieut Col. H.P. CREAGH-OSBORNE The King's Own Regt assumed command of the Battalion.	
	Relieved from French Duty by 4/5" Bn Loyal North Lanc. Regt. The Battalion going into Reserve Billets at FLEURBAIX.	
	Casualties, Wounded one O.R. Died 1. O.R.	
do 10/4/17	Took over French Duty from the 4/5 Bn Loyal North Lanc. Regt.	
do 17/4/17	Casualties, Wounded, one O.R.	
do 20/4/17	Casualties, Killed, one O.R Wounded one O.R.	
do 22/4/17	Casualties, Killed, two O.Rs	
do 24/4/17	Relieved from French Duty by the 4/5 "Bn Loyal North Lancs Regt. Battalion going into Reserve Billets at FLEURBAIX.	

H Creagh Osborne
COLONEL.
O.C. 2/5th BN. THE KING'S OWN R. LANCASTER REGT.

WAR DIARY

or INTELLIGENCE SUMMARY

Army Form C. 2118

2/5th THE KING'S OWN R. LANC. REGT.

MAY 1917

(Erase heading not required.)

Place	Date	Hour	Summary of Events and Information	Remarks and references to Appendices
BOUTILLERIE SECTOR	2/5/17		Relieved the 4/5th Bn Loyal North Lancashire Regt in BOUTILLERIE TRENCH SECTOR	7b/
do	2/5/17		Casualties:- Wounded 4 O.Rs.	7b/
do	3/5/17		Casualties:- Wounded, Capt R.H. HARVEY and 1. O.R.	7b/
do	7/5/17		Casualties:- Wounded, 1. O.R.	7b/
do	8/5/17		**Casualties:- Wounded, 3. O.R.**	7b/ 7b/
do	10/5/17		Casualties:- Wounded, 1. O.R.	7b/
do	10/5/17		Relieved from Trench duty by the 4/5th Loyal North Lancs Regt. The Battalion going into reserve billets at FLEURBAIX.	7b/
FLEURBAIX	12/5/17		Casualties:- Died, 1 O.R.	7b/
BOUTILLERIE SECTOR	17/5/17		Took over trench duty in the BOUTILLERIE SECTOR relieving 4/5 Loyal North Lancs Regt	7b/ 7b/
do	18/5/17		Casualties:- Wounded 1 O.R.	7b/
do	19/5/17		No 240595 Pte DENNISON awarded the Military medal.	7b/
do	19/5/17		Casualties:- Wounded 2. O.Rs.	7b/
do	20/5/17		Casualties:- Wounded 1. O.R.	7b/
do	21/5/17		Casualties:- Wounded 3. O.Rs.	7b/
do	23/5/17		Casualties:- Died of wounds 1 O.R. Wounded 3. O.Rs.	7b/
do	24/5/17		Casualties:- Died of wounds 1 O.R. att to 1/1st L.T.M.B.	7b/
do	25/5/17		Casualties:- Wounded 1. O.R.	7b/
do	25/5/17		Relieved from Trench duty by the 4/5th Loyal Lancashire Regt & Bn going into reserve billets FLEURBAIX.	7b/

CONFIDENTIAL

WAR DIARY or INTELLIGENCE SUMMARY

Army Form C. 2118

2/5 The King's Own R. Lanc. Regt.

JUNE 1917

Instructions regarding War Diaries and Intelligence Summaries are contained in F.S. Regs., Part II. and the Staff Manual respectively. Title Pages will be prepared in manuscript.

Place	Date	Hour	Summary of Events and Information	Remarks and references to Appendices
BOUTILLERIE FRENCH SECTOR	2-6-17		Took over duty in the trenches BOUTILLERIE SECTOR relieving 4/5th Loyal North Lancs Regt	
	3-6-17		Casualties. Killed 2 O.Rs. Wounded 1 O.R.	
	5-6-17		Casualties. Wounded 2/Lt F.A. TOTSUM slightly on duty, and 3 O.Rs.	
	7-6-17		Casualties. Wounded. 2 O.Rs.	
	8-6-17		Casualties. Wounded. 1 O.R.	
	10-6-17		Casualties. Wounded 2 O.Rs	
	10-6-17		Relieved from trench duty by the 4/5 Loyal North Lanc. Regt. The Battalion being employed in FLEURBAIX	
	17-6-17		Took over duty in the trenches relieving the 4/5 Loyal North Lanc Regt	
	17-6-17		Casualties. Wounded. 2 O.Rs.	
	18-6-17		Casualties. Wounded. 1 O.R.	
	19-6-17		Casualties. Wounded. 1 O.R.	
	21-6-17		Casualties. Wounded. 2 O.Rs	
	22-6-17		Casualties. Wounded of 1 O.R.	
	22-6-17		On the night of the 22/23 a patrol of one officer & 19 O.Rs. under 2/Lt WHALEY, entered the German trenches near HERRBAIX. The Patrol proceeded along the trench on each side for a short distance but finding all the O.Ts. unmanned and with no Germans in sight the Patrol broke up into 3 return parties. Falling back two were tackled on their return the enemy, having been attracted by a party wondering too much in the open. The enemy were tackled with rifle and bomb. Our party returned to our lines without casualties of any sort.	
	23-6-17		Casualties. Wounded 4 O.Rs.	

WAR DIARY or INTELLIGENCE SUMMARY

Army Form C. 2118

2/5th The King's Own Royal Lancaster Regt.

JULY 1917

Place	Date	Hour	Summary of Events and Information	Remarks and references to Appendices
BOUTILLERIE TRENCH SECTOR	1-7-17		Casualties: Wounded 2nd Lt. F.P. GODFREY and 1 O.R. (both accidental)	
	2-7-17		Awards: No. 2702 Pte. J.K. BELL and No. 242146 Pte. R. KERSHAW (late 2/5th Loyals) were awarded the MILITARY MEDAL for gallantry and devotion to duty in action. (Cas. of award 2/5/17)	
FLEURBAIX			(Entry:- XI Corps Routine Order No.1780 (2) dated 26/6/17)	
	3-7-17		Casualties: Wounded 1 O.R. injury (accidental)	
	4-7-17		Casualties: wounded 1 O.R.	
	5-7-17		Casualties: Killed 1 O.R. Wounded 1 O.R.	
	6-7-17		Casualties: Wounded 1 O.R.	
	7-7-17		Casualties: Wounded 6 O.R.	
	15-7-17		Relieved from Trenches by 1st Bn 4/5th South York Regt. and the night of 8/14 July. 2nd Lieutenant Jenny and 3 Lieut. Robles on FLEUREAN	
			Took over Left Sub-Sector of relief of M.G.C. 142nd Brigade on June 15/16	
	17/7/17		Casualties: Wounded 2/Lt E.T. WHALLEY & 2 O.R.	
	18/7/17		Casualties: Wounded 1 O.R.	
	19/7/17		Casualties: Died of wounds 1 O.R.	
	21/7/17		Casualties: Killed 1 O.R. Wounded 2/Lt E.H. SMITH + 4 O.Rs	
	22/7/17		Casualties: Wounded 1 O.R.	
	23/7/17		Relieved from Trench Sub by the 4/5th Loyal North Lancs Regt. The Batln. going into Reserve	
	25/7/17		Casualties: - Killed 1 O.R.	
	31/7/17		Casualties: - Wounded 2/Lt. E.C. [?]	
			Relieved from Reserve to BOUTILLERIE SECTOR by the 12th LEICESTER REGT. Proceeded to HOUPLINES SECTOR, ARMENTIERES by motor lorries. Two companies in Billets & ARMENTIERES, two Coys at Subsidiary line HOUPLINES SECTOR.	

S E C R E T.

Headquarters,
170th. Infantry Brigade.

Herewith War Diary for the month of August 1917 in respect of this Unit, for your information.

In the Field.
1/9/17.

W W Morrell Capt & adj
for
Major,
Commanding,
2/5th. Bn. THE KING'S OWN R.L.R.

Army Form C. 2118.

WAR DIARY
or
INTELLIGENCE SUMMARY

(Erase heading not required.)

2/5- The KING'S OWN ROYAL LANCASTER Regt.

AUGUST 1917

Instructions regarding War Diaries and Intelligence Summaries are contained in F.S. Regs., Part II. and the Staff Manual respectively. Title pages will be prepared in manuscript.

Hour, Date, Place	Summary of Events and Information	Remarks and references to Appendices
HOOPLINES TRENCH SECTOR 1/8/17 ARMENTIERES	Relieved the 2/7th KINGS LIVERPOOL Regt. from trench duty in this sector by the 1/72.	
do 2/8/17	Casualties:- Wounded 3. O.Rs.	
do 3/8/17	Casualties:- Killed 1. O.R. Wounded 10. ORs	
5/8/17	Casualties:- Wounded 4. O.Rs	
6/8/17	Casualties:- 2/Lieut. A.P. GODFREY and 1. A.J.GT.S. wounded (gassed)	
	4 O.Rs. wounded and 39 O.R. missed (gassed)	
14/8/17	Relieved from trench duty in the trenches by the 4/5th R. Royal Fort. Lancs. Regt. 2/5 Battalion going into reserve ARMENTIERES.	
14/8/17	Casualties: Killed 1 O.R. Wounded 2 O.Rs.	
15/8/17	Casualties:- Wounded 1. O.R.	
17/8/17	Casualties:- Wounded 2. O.Rs	
18/8/17	Casualties:- Wounded 1. O.R.	
21/8/17	Relieved the 4/5th R. Royal Lancs. Regt. in HOOPLINES SECTOR, relieving to 5/8. Royal Lancs. Regt. in support.	
21/8/17	Casualties:- Wounded 4. O.Rs.	
22/8/17	Casualties:- Killed 1 O.R. Wounded 1/6 STONEHOUSE and 5 ORs	
23/8/17	Casualties:- Wounded 3 O.Rs	
25/8/17	Casualties:- Killed 1. O.R. Wounded 3 O.Rs	
26/8/17	Casualties:- Died of wounds 1 O.R.	
	Relieved from trench duty by the 1/5th Royal Tank Lancs. Regt. the Battalion going into reserve in ARMENTIERES.	

F Howard Major
O.C. 2/5th Bn. THE KING'S OWN R. LANCASTER REGT.

Army Form C. 2118.

WAR DIARY
INTELLIGENCE SUMMARY

(Erase heading not required.)

2/5 Bn. THE KING'S OWN. ROYAL LANCASTER REGT.

SEPTEMBER 1917

Instructions regarding War Diaries and Intelligence Summaries are contained in F.S. Regs., Part II. and the Staff Manual respectively. Title pages will be prepared in manuscript.

Hour, Date, Place	Summary of Events and Information	Remarks and references to Appendices
1 September 1917 ARMENTIERES	Casualties: 1 O.R.	
2 — HOUPLINES TRENCH SECTOR ARMENTIERES	Took over trench duty in the HOUPLINES SECTOR, relieving the 4/5 Loyal N. Lancs.	
3rd do do do	North Lancs. Regt. Casualties 1 O.R. wounded.	
5th do do do	Casualties:— Killed 1 O.R.	
6th do do do		
4.20 to 5.0, 6/9/17 do do	Casualties:— Killed, 2 O.Rs. Wounded, 15 O.Rs. Missing 1 O.R. During a heavy bombardment, the enemy approached the M21 Post at the back of LONDON ROAD and gained a footing in our trenches from which they were ejected after a sharp fight. The papers on these dead Germans taken in our lines shew the identity/colour to be normal. The troops opposed belong to the 8th Company (2nd Bn.) 8th Bavarian I.R.	
7 Sept 1917 HOUPLINES TRENCH SECTOR	Casualties: 1 O.R. wounded	
8 Sept 1917 do	Casualties:— 2/Lt. T.H.N. SPENCER (att. from 1/4 K.W.L.R.) wounded (gas)	
9 Sept 1917 do	During the night of the 8/9 the enemy attempted to exit our lines in two places. A strong enemy raiding party attempted to enter our line immediately S. of the RYS at 11.30 p.m. but were driven off. Our sentries followed the enemy back and after 1st to overtake the raiders not succeed. Enemy's losses proved small. At 2.10am a second raid was attempted by the enemy s. of London Road further S. This raid was also driven off. It is said a third raid was also unsuccessful, made a little to our right. It has not been to return the female raided wards in the night. Our casualties from all sources were — Killed, 3 O.Rs and Wounded, — 8 O.Rs.	
10 Sept HOUPLINES SECTOR do	Casualties:— 7 O.Rs.	
11 Sept do	Relieved from HOUPLINES SECTOR by the 1/5 Bn. The Loyal N. Lancs. Regt. Battalion billeted in ARMENTIERES	

Army Form C. 2118.

WAR DIARY
or
INTELLIGENCE SUMMARY

(Erase heading not required.)

SEPTEMBER 1917

Instructions regarding War Diaries and Intelligence Summaries are contained in F. S. Regs.; Part II. and the Staff Manual respectively. Title pages will be prepared in manuscript.

Hour, Date, Place	Summary of Events and Information	Remarks and references to Appendices
1.10 a.m. 16/9/17 ARMENTIERES	Relieved from Reserve to the HOUPLINES TRENCH SECTOR by the 17th Bn. Royal Welsh Fusiliers. The Batt. proceeded by road route to DE SEULE CAMP, NIEPPE arriving at 4.30 a.m.	
8.47 a.m. 18/9/17 DE SEULE CAMP NIEPPE	Left by March Route for training area at AUCHY-AU-BOIS arrived at Bast CH de DUVELLE in MERVILLE were the troops were billeted for the night.	
18/9/17 CH. DUVELLE		
19/9/17 L'ECLÈME near LILLERS	Continued march to training area. Troops billeted for the night in and around L'ECLÈME on the LILLERS - ROBECQ ROAD	
20/9/17 AUCHY-AU-BOIS	Continued march and arrived at AUCHY. (T14 d Map FRANCE Sheet 36 A) by noon. troops billeted. Lt. Col. J.J. CAMERON assumed command of the Battalion, in place of Lt. Col. M.R. CRESAGH-OSBORNE who proceeded to England.	
21/9/17 AUCHY-AU-BOIS	Training began.	

J.W. [signed] Major for L.Col.
Comdg. 2/5 R.W. Fusiliers. 1/9/17

CONFIDENTIAL.

Headquarters,
170th. Infantry Brigade.
_____

Herewith War Diary for the month of October, 1917 in respect of this unit, for your information.

[signature] Lt.Colonel,
Commanding,
2/5th. Bn. The King's Own R.L.Regt.

In the Field.
1.11.1917.

Army Form C. 2118.

Vol 9
170
5-7

WAR DIARY

2/5 THE KING'S OWN ROYAL LANCASTER REGT.

INTELLIGENCE SUMMARY

October 1917

(Erase heading not required.)

Hour, Date, Place	Summary of Events and Information	Remarks and references to Appendices
1st October. AUCHY AU BOIS	Training and recreation.	Nil
6 October. AUCHY AU BOIS	The Battalion was inspected by the Field Marshal Sir Douglas Haig K.T. G.C.B, &c C in C British Armies in France - the Batt. was formed up in Mass. on the RELY - ESTRÉE BLANCHE Road.	Nil
7 October. ENGUINEGATE	Brigade Training	Nil
17 October. AUCHY AU BOIS	7th Battalion moved by Tracl. Route to COIN PERDU east of ST-OMER.	Nil
18 October. COIN PERDU	7th Battalion proceeded by Buss Route to PROVEN and then by Tracl. Route to PENTON CAMP arriving at 6-45 p.m.	Nil
22 October. PENTON CAMP PROVEN BELGIUM	Received training. Orders to move to forward area on Oct 23rd to MARSOUIN F.M. Area.	Nil
23 October. PENTON CAMP	Proceeded by train from PROVEN to ELVERDINGHE and then by March Route to WOLF CAMP. Three officers + 510 O.R.s moved by March Route to Corps Reinforcement Camp at HERZEELE	Nil
24 October. WOLF CAMP ELVERDINGHE	At 4 p.m. the Battalion less one Company moved forward to EAGLE TRENCH as Support Battalion to the 170 Inf. Brigade, covering the 2/d Bn Northumberland Fusrs.	Nil
9 p.m. 25 October. EAGLE TRENCH SCHREIBOOM to POELCAPPELLE	A, B. + C Companies moved from EAGLE TRENCH at 9 p.m. proceeding by Track "A" to CONFRONIS farm arriving there about 11.30 p.m. The line WATERHOUSE farm - CONFRONIS farm had been reconnoitred and was chosen as the forming up line. copy SHAAP BALIE MAP. 1/10 000 Edition 1	Nil

Army Form C. 2118.

Sheet 2

OCTOBER 1917

WAR DIARY
of
INTELLIGENCE SUMMARY
2/5 The King's Own Royal LANCASTER Regt
(Erase heading not required.)

Instructions regarding War Diaries and Intelligence Summaries are contained in F. S. Regs., Part II. and the Staff Manual respectively. Title pages will be prepared in manuscript.

Hour, Date, Place	Summary of Events and Information	Remarks and references to Appendices
NARRATIVE OF OPERATIONS ON 26 October 1917 SHAAP BALIE	Ref:- SHAAP-BALIE Map 1/10,000 Edition 1	

The battalion became one company were detailed as Support Battalion to 170th Brigade, with orders to follow the attacking battalion at a distance of 300x take up a position in the neighbourhood of MEMLING from and assist all nuisance occurrences to the attacking battalions.

The three companies "H", "B", & "C" Coys moved from ERNIE TRENCH at 9 p.m. on the 25th Oct. preceded by "A" Coys to COMPRENIS farm and concentrated about 11.30 p.m.

The line WATERHOUSE farm - COMPRENIS farm had been reconnoitred and was chosen as the forming up line and was in magnificent. Companies forming some road. Direction was held by compass bearing by Commanders P" to task to BESAGE farm was from and as not felt to assure that as companies would eventually reach the neighbourhood of MEMLING from the left company west of the WATERVLIET-BREEK a good deal left from a complete part of the liaison from 171st and 172nd Inf'y Brigades from and in front left Coys tried told off to keep level and touch 45.

Direction was kept by Coys owners to any weed support and as experience showed having attracted the direction from the attacking battalion is the Companies advanced past confused from the enemy barrage. About 300x in order to avoid the enemy barrage.

As centre Coy H.Q. and reserve platoon took up a position 300 W. of MEMLING farm on arrival, using forward offering no expection field of fire E and S.E. the platoon reinforced 2/4 L.N.L Regt forward, 3rd platoon in front of MEMLING.

Sheet 5

Army Form C. 2118.

WAR DIARY
or
INTELLIGENCE SUMMARY

2/5" The KING'S OWN ROYAL LANCASTER Regt.
(Erase heading not required.)

OCTOBER 1917

Hour, Date, Place	Summary of Events and Information	Remarks and references to Appendices
	Right Company placed from advance about 100" S. of MEMLING, covering a gap which existed between the south and right Battalions of the attacking line. The line leading N.E. from N. of this Coy. reinforced by the attacking Battalion about 300 E. of MEMLING. The Left Company found that the WATERVLIETBEEK was fordable in places so no platoon crossed and continued forward of the N. side of it, some sections formed a defensive flank in the neighbourhood of GRAVEL farm. That of the attacking line who were back to their positions were now pushed thro'. A counter attack on the left was broken up by rifle and Lewis Gun fire. The guns in charge of the platoon 100" S. of MEMLING farm was shelled the house on its support were seen approaching and acted with coolness & were able to cover Battalion who were through. Bn. Headquarters moved up to new [?] on position on the north of Public Embankment as reported up. Smoke had established the H.Q. advanced to [?] [?] on its [?] an outpost. The Right Coy. cond. M.L.R. [?] on our right attacking [?] for repelling any further attack. The Royal North Lancs. Bn. on our right had no officers in command, M.O.s, and our Right Coy. had lost 2 Lieut. Junior Officers, the 1/4th Bn. Commander therefore recognised of R.N Lancs was in a [?] and night. The obstruction of the advance of neighbours [?] [?] Left Coy. somewhat contained on account of groups forming a defensive flank near GRAVEL farm. The Centre Coy.	

Sheet 4

Army Form C. 2118.

WAR DIARY
or
INTELLIGENCE SUMMARY

2/5 The King's Own Royal Lancaster Regt.
(Erase heading not required.)

October 1917

Hour, Date, Place	Summary of Events and Information	Remarks and references to Appendices
27 October 3 p.m. PITCHCOTT CAMP PROVEN AREA No.1.	The Centre Coy near BOWER HOUSE, the Right Coy and the Royal Naval Div on a line from BESAGE farm to REQUETE farm. They rejoined the position and relieved during the night 26/27 October by the 2/5 King's Own R. Regt. Our casualties during the Operations were:— Killed: 2/Lt S.H. WOOD and 2/Lt R.E. BENNET and B. E O. Rs. Wounded: 2nd Lieuts K. FARQUHARSON, O. COTTON, F. IBBOTSON, J.G. BLAKE and 130 O. Ru. Ranks. Missing: 33 O.Rs. Ranks.	H
28 October 1917 RITCHCOTT CAMP PROVEN BELGIUM	The Battalion assembled at POSE Camp and was forwarded by Motor Buses to BOESINGHE Station, and there entrained to PROVEN.	H
	Reorganisation of Battalion commenced.	H
29 October 1917 5.0 a.m RITCHCOTT CAMP PROVEN.	A Composite Platoon of 1 Officer & 38 O.Rs left camp to form a carrying party to Artillery near PILKEM.	H
30 October 1917 7.0 a m PITCHCOTT CAMP PROVEN.	"D" Company proceeded to FISHMILLER HOUSE, H.Q. 179 Inf Brigade to act as Carrying party to upper Gunners.	H

Forward by Colonel
J.R. Hastings Commanding
Colonel
J.R. Hastings Commanding
2/5 The King's Own R.L.R.

1247 W 3299 200,000 (E) 8/14 J.B.C. & A. Forms/C. 2118/11.

Headquarters,
    170th Infantry Brigade.
_____

        Herewith War Diary for the month of
November, 1917, in respect of this unit for your
information.

                        H. Seward   Major,
                                     Commanding,
1/12/17.   2/5th Bn The King's Own R.L.R.

> 2/5TH BATTALION,
> THE KING'S OWN
> R.L.R.
> No. 986
> Date 1/12/17

Army Form C. 2118.

WAR DIARY
or
INTELLIGENCE SUMMARY
2/5 THE KING'S OWN R Lancs Regt
(Erase heading not required.)

NOVEMBER 1917

Instructions regarding War Diaries and Intelligence Summaries are contained in F.S. Regs., Part II. and the Staff Manual respectively. Title pages will be prepared in manuscript.

Hour, Date, Place	Summary of Events and Information	Remarks and references to Appendices
11:30am 4 Nov PROVEN BELGIUM	Inspection of the Battalion and Coy's by the Army Commander, V ARMY.	7&1
6.30am 8th Nov PITCHCOTT CAMP PROVEN	The Battalion entrained for ARDRUICQ and then marched to the training area at SANGHEM and ALEMBON near LICQUES - FRANCE	7&1
9th Nov SANGHEM, FRANCE	Received draft of 97 other ranks	7&1
11th Nov SANGHEM in LICQUES	Increase in strength by 2 Officers & 29 O.Rs (Lieuts J.E.DUIGEMAN & C.R.HARGREAVES) 7&1	
14 Nov SANGHEM	Lectures on "Trench Feet" to all Officers & NCOs by the A.D.M.S.	7&1
13th Nov SANGHEM	Received a draft of six other ranks	7&1
21 Nov SANGHEM	Commanding Officer, 2nd i/c & the O.C. Coy's attended lectures by Corps Commander XVIII Corps on Training	7&1
27 Nov SANGHEM	Lectures by Brigadier G.O.C Brigade on Methods of Instruction and the new formation for Attack.	7&1
28 Nov SANGHEM	Recognition Cards awarded to the following for gallant conduct in action on the 26th Oct 1917	7&1
30 Nov SANGHEM	The Military Medal was awarded for gallant conduct and devotion to duty in action on the 26th Oct 1917, to the following: 241313 ½ CARNEY E 7&1 24/101 Sgt CROMPTON W, 240536 Sgt RUNDLE W. 16622 L/C WARDRICK W. 240726 Pte WILCOCK J. 4921 Sgt HALLIWELL R. 220672 Sgt BOAGAR J.N 241236 Pte PARR W. 28678 Pte CALBY F. 241842 Pte FREARA. 82660 Pte FRANCE T 202288 Pte BOTTSWORTH W. 241305 Pte WERRITT S. 240642 Pte HARGREAVES J. 241137 Cpl GOODWIN E. 241259 Pte GOODWIN E	

1247 W 8299 200,000 (E) 8/14 J.B.C. & A. Forms/C. 2118/11.

Army Form C. 2118.

19 DECEMBER 1917 WAR DIARY or INTELLIGENCE SUMMARY

Instructions regarding War Diaries and Intelligence Summaries are contained in F. S. Regs., Part II. and the Staff Manual respectively. Title pages will be prepared in manuscript.

(Erase heading not required.) 2/5th The KING'S OWN R. LANCS Regt.

Hour, Date, Place	Summary of Events and Information	Remarks and references to Appendices
SANGHEM FRANCE Map Ref. CALAIS 13 Jan edn 1/12/17	The Battalion out–711th line fire trainery	
GUEMY FRANCE Map Ref. HAZEBROUCK 5A 7/12/17	Brigade training, attack formations	
SANGHEM FRANCE 9/12/17	The Battn moved by Buses to POODLE and PITCHCOTT Camps CANADA AREA PROVEN, BELGIUM. (Map Ref HAZEBROUCK SA. – 2 I 15.66)	
PROVEN. 12/12/17	Proceeded by March. Routs to BAPAUME CAMP. HARINGHE – ROUSBRUGGE (Map Ref. HAZEBROUCK J" 2.H 45 95)	
BAPAUME CAMP 15/12/17	The Camp was inspected by the Divisional General; (report good) lecture to all officers by G.O.C. Brigade.	
BAPAUME CAMP 16/12/17	Two Companies A + B detached for work with the 173 Tunnelling Coy at DROMORE CORNER (A.18.a.9.4. Belgium 28NW) Battalion HQ and "C" and "D" Coys moved by march route to H CAMP (A.10.a.0.2 Belgium 28 NW).	
17/12/17 H. CAMP (A.10.a.0.2)	6 hours gun teams proceeded to forward area so to take over Anti-Aircraft positions from 18th Division.	
H. CAMP 18/12/17	Casualties S. OR wounded in forward area.	
H. CAMP 19/12/17	"C" + "D" Coys detached for work with 173 Tunnelling Coy at DROMORE CORNER (A.18. a. 9.4. Belgium 28 NW)	

Army Form C. 2118

WAR DIARY
or
INTELLIGENCE SUMMARY
(Erase heading not required.)

Instructions regarding War Diaries and Intelligence Summaries are contained in F. S. Regs., Part II. and the Staff Manual respectively. Title Pages. will be prepared in manuscript.

Place	Date	Hour	Summary of Events and Information	Remarks and references to Appendices
20th "H" Camp	20/12/17		Major S. E. Ball MC assumes command vice Major F. W. Seward (Leave)	
"H" Camp	22/12/17		Casualties 2 OR killed & 4 OR wounded in Forward Area	
"H" Camp	25/12/17		Christmas Day – All ranks spent an enjoyable time, contributed to by liberal rations and the generosity of friends of the battalion	
"H" Camp	29/12/17		A portion of each company working with the 173 Tunnelling Coy return to H Camp	
H Camp	30/12/17		The remainder of each company working with the 173 Tunnelling Co return to H Camp	
PETWORTH CAMP (Sheet 9 x.25.d.n.y)	31/12/17	9.35am	Proceeded by March Route to PETWORTH CAMP	

L. C. Ball Major
2/5th 9th Royal Sussex Regt

Army Form C. 2118.

WAR DIARY
or
INTELLIGENCE SUMMARY

(Erase heading not required.)

Summary of Events and Information

WAR DIARY.

2/5th. Bn. THE KING'S OWN (ROYAL LANCASTER) REGT.

JANUARY 1918.

Army Form C. 2118.

WAR DIARY
or
INTELLIGENCE SUMMARY

(Erase heading not required.)

January 1918

Instructions regarding War Diaries and Intelligence Summaries are contained in F.S. Regs., Part II. and the Staff Manual respectively. Title pages will be prepared in manuscript.

Hour, Date, Place	Summary of Events and Information	Remarks and references to Appendices
Petworth Camp 1.1.18	Lt Col J.J. Cameron D.S.O. resumed command on return from leave	
Petworth Camp 2.1.18 8.0 am	Proceeded to PROVEN STATION entrained. Detrained at BAILLEUL and marched to WATERLANDS CAMP (B9210 b0 Sh28 36 NW.) Joined I ANZAC CORPS	
Waterlands Camp 3.1.18	Proceeded by March Route to take over the CHAPELLE SECTOR of trenches in the ARMENTIÈRES Cushion. B.H.Q. (I14d 45.70 Sheet 36 NW)	
CHAPELLE Sector 8.1.18 3.30	2Lt Thompson with a patrol of 5 OR entered E.P.L. & secured a prisoner	
CHAPELLE Sector 9.1.18 (renamed MEZ MACQUART)	Handed over to 4/5" Batt Loyal North Lancs. proceeded to billets in ERQUINGHEM (H.14.d. 05.45 - 36NW) Less C.o.B Coys to LA ROLANDERIE (H.11.d.60.60)	
15.1.18. ERQUINGHEM.	Relieved the 2/5th Batt. L.N.L. in close support. 3 Companies in the subsidiary line of the Brigade sector (MEZ MACQUART.) 1 Coy in the FLEURIE SWITCH. B.H.Q at ARTILLERY FARM. (H.7.d 40.30. 36NW)	
20.1.18.	Handed over to 2/5 Batt L.N.L. & proceeded to their billets in ERQUINGHEM & LA ROLANDERIE FARM. (the Soldiers of the Support Battn)	
23.1.18. —	3 day reliefs notified. owing to ——— condition of trenches after the thaw. Relieved 2/5 L.N.L in CLOSE SUPPORT	
26.1.18 —	Handed over to 2/5" L.N.L. moving to SUPPORT BILLETS.	
29.1.18 —	Back to CLOSE SUPPORT relieving 2/5 L.N.L.	
17.1.18	MAJOR S.C. SHELMC ———— Command of Battn. in the absence on Special Leave of Lt-Col. W. Crompton D.S.O. M.C.	
HONOURS & AWARDS.	NEW YEAR 1918. LT-COL CAMERON D.S.O. awarded M.C. 240077 - Q.S.M MARK NEWTON D.C.M.	
	MENTIONS MAJOR F.R. SHARD. CAPT (A/MAJOR) M.W. SINKERTHWAITE (2nd) 4/5LN.D. A/CAPT. R. EDWARDS. LIEUT. P.H. DELAFIELD.	

Army Form C. 2118.

WAR DIARY
or
INTELLIGENCE SUMMARY

(Erase heading not required.)

JANUARY 1918.

Hour, Date, Place	Summary of Events and Information	Remarks and references to Appendices
HONOURS & AWARDS.	(1) 2/Lieut D. HEW YEAR. 241060 PTE ALLDAY G.B.	
21.1.18	267. H THOMPSON Awarded M.C. for the Patrol more on 81/18.	
	A very quiet month. Very little hostile activity. During the time the Batn (& Brigade) has been in this Sector all efforts have been turned on to the improvement of old & permanent new defences. The trenches have been manned very lightly. Old trenches & shelters have in some cases been blown up & no very effective use is being	
	31.1.18	
CASUALTIES	1.1.18 W. 1. O.R.
	4.1.18 W. 1. O.R. (acc)
	24.1.18 W. 2. O.R. (1 since D. of W.)

B.A. Paul
Capt. & Adjt.
for Major Commanding
2/5. Bn. The King's Own (R.L.) Regiment

Army Form C. 2118.

WAR DIARY
or
INTELLIGENCE SUMMARY

(Erase heading not required.)

Summary of Events and Information

Hour, Date, Place

Remarks and references to Appendices

WAR DIARY

2/5 Batt. THE KING'S OWN R. LANC. REG^T

FEBRUARY 1917

Instructions regarding War Diaries and Intelligence Summaries are contained in F. S. Regs.; Part II. and the Staff Manual respectively. Title pages will be prepared in manuscript.

WAR DIARY or INTELLIGENCE SUMMARY

Army Form C. 2118.

(Erase heading not required.)

Hour, Date, Place	Summary of Events and Information	Remarks and references to Appendices
Reference – France 36 1:40,000		
ERQUINGHEM 1/2/18 (H.4.d.1.4)	Battalion in Support in billets, finding Working parties daily	
HOLLEBECQUE CAMP 5/2/18 (B.19.b.8.7) 50	Battalion proceeded to HOLLEBECQUE CAMP as Battⁿ in Reserve. Training on	
7/2/18	5 Officers & 126 O.R. transferred to this Battⁿ	
WEZ MACQUART SECTION 9/2/18 (I.14.d.4.8)	Battⁿ proceeded to the WEZ MACQUART Section of trenches which they took over from the 1/5th Battⁿ Royal North Lancashire Regt	
11/2/18 3.0 am	"B" Coy attempted a raid on the enemy trenches at I.21.c.15.05 and I.21.c.45.20 with two platoons under 2.Lt Thompson & 2.Lt Elliot. The intention was that the raid should bear been a silent one with the Artillery, Trench Mortars and MGs standing by. On our Raiding Parties arriving at the Enemy's wire, rifle & machine gun fire was opened & bombs thrown by the enemy who were very alert. The O/c Raid in consequence signalled to the Artillery who together with the Trench Mortars & Machine Guns opened fire at 3.4 a.m. & continued till 3.40 a.m. The hostile artillery & trench mortars also opened fire a few minutes later. It was not possible to enter the enemy trenches & the parties returned when the artillery quietened down. Capt. Austin, 2.Lt Thompson & S.M Swades of B Coy & Capt Perl the Regiment afterwards assisted men staying in NML to regain our trenches. Casualties 2 missing 12 wounded (3 remained at duty)	

Army Form C. 2118.

WAR DIARY (2)
or
INTELLIGENCE SUMMARY
(Erase heading not required.)

Instructions regarding War Diaries and Intelligence Summaries are contained in F. S. Regs., Part II. and the Staff Manual respectively. Title pages will be prepared in manuscript.

Hour, Date, Place	Summary of Events and Information	Remarks and references to Appendices
Reference – France 36ᴬ 1:40,000		
ESTAIRES L.30,b,2.9 13/2/18	Battⁿ relieved by 14 Battⁿ Royal Welsh Fusiliers & proceeded by march to ERQUINGHEM (H,4,a,4.4) & by lorry to ESTAIRES Billeted in the Brewery. 2 Rounders Battalion	
ST HILAIRE T.5.d.5.8 14/2/18	Battⁿ proceeded by lorry to ST HILAIRE where they occupied billets.	
" 15/2/18 – 28/2/18	Training	
" 16/2/18	Reinforcement of 20 O.R.	
" 18/2/18	Col. D.J. Cameron D.S.O., M.C. resumes command on return from sick leave.	
" 21/2/18	Reinforcement of 99 O.R.	
" 25/2/18	The G.O.C. 59ᵗʰ Division inspected the Battⁿ & expressed himself very pleased with the general bearing & turn out.	
" 26/2/18	H.M. the King has approved the award of :– The Croix de Guerre (Belgium) to C.S.M. Swaites A.E. The Decoration Militaire " " " to R/6 Bouthwaite W.6.	
" 27/2/18	The G.O.C. XV Corps inspected the 170ᵗʰ Infᵗʳʸ Brigade, and presented the following decorations to Officers & Other Ranks of this Battⁿ being immediate awards earned during the period 24/10/17 – 26/10/17 Military Cross – – – – – Major S.E. Ball, 2ⁿᵈ Lieut W. Thompson (5/11/18) Military Medal – – – – – Sgt. Rundle, Sgt. Wilcock, Sgt. Benson Cpl. Warbrick, Pte. Baley, Trer. Frazer, R/6 Carney, R/6 Wrerill, Ronson	

S E C R E T.

Headquarters,
    170th. Infantry Brigade.
_____

    Herewith War Diary for the month of March in respect of this Unit for your information.

                                    [signature] Major
                                    for. Lt.Colonel,
                                        Commanding,
31.3.1918.   2/5th. Bn. The King's Own R.L.R.

ORIGINAL   MARCH 1918   2nd/5th KING'S OWN ROYAL LANCASTER REGT.
Army Form C. 2118.

WAR DIARY or INTELLIGENCE SUMMARY

(Erase heading not required.)

Instructions regarding War Diaries and Intelligence Summaries are contained in F.S. Regs., Part II. and the Staff Manual respectively. Title pages will be prepared in manuscript.

Hour, Date, Place	Summary of Events and Information	Remarks and references to Appendices
8.15 a.m. 1/3/18. ST. HILAIRE	Battalion moved to LE SART	
12 noon 2/3/18 LE SART	Battalion moved to ESTAIRES (S) area. Temporarily attached to 172nd Inf. Brigade.	
12 noon 10/3/18 ESTAIRES	Battalion moved to NEUF BERQUIN - DOULIEU area. (36a E 9.c.00.00) Returned to 176th Inf. Bde.	
16/3/18 MERVILLE	1. O.R. wounded.	
5.h.m. NEUF BERQUIN 19/3/18	Battalion Hdqrs. Lewis for the line.	
2.50 a.m. BOIS GRENIER 20/3/18.	Battalion relieved 9th Bn. Royal West Kent Regt. in the line in BOIS GRENIER Sector. Transport shelled on road. One man wounded on road. Transfers intermittently shelled also. Casualties Lieut. T.K.S. BALDWIN & 2 O.R. killed 5 O.R. wounded	
12.15 a.m. BOIS GRENIER 21/3/18 12.15 a.m.	Enemy attempted to raid left post of right company, but was repulsed with losses. Our rifle fire. Intermittent shelling. Casualties Wounded 2 O.R.	
22/3/18	Gas shelling on right Coy. Left Coy. intermittently shelled and minning. Trench Mortars were fired on right company. Casualties Killed 1 O.R. Wounded 1 O.R.	

1247. W 3209. 200,000. (E) 8/14. J.B.C. & A.   Forms/C. 2118/11.

ORIGINAL 2ND/5TH KING'S OWN ROYAL LANCASTER REG

MARCH 1918

Army Form C. 2118

WAR DIARY
or
INTELLIGENCE SUMMARY
(Erase heading not required.)

Instructions regarding War Diaries and Intelligence Summaries are contained in F.S. Regs., Part II. and the Staff Manual respectively. Title Pages will be prepared in manuscript.

Place	Date	Hour	Summary of Events and Information	Remarks and references to Appendices
BOIS GRENIER	March 25		Enemy artillery active on battalion front. Trench mortars active on right company front. Casualties 1 O.R. wounded (at duty.)	
" "	26	4.55 a.m.	Enemy attempted to raid our right post held by men of "C" Coy. Strength of enemy estimated at 30. Enemy attacked in extended formation but were beaten off by rapid fire stand and bombs thrown by the garrison. A dead German was brought in belonging to 371st Infantry Regiment. 10th Ersatz Division. Remainder of days operations by enemy. We had a few men slightly wounded. Casualties 4 O.R. wounded.	
" "	25		Evening quiet day. Casualties 1 O.R. wounded.	
" "	N-Spr 26/27		Very quiet day. Battalion was relieved in line by 2/17th King's Liverpool Regiment & proceeded to rear billets in NOUVEAU MONDE & SAILLY SUR LA LYS.	
NOUVEAU MONDE	27		Reconnaissance carried out in forward area and working parties supplied for work on 2nd and Corps line Defences.	
" "	29	8 h.m.	Battalion left billets & marched to EROUINGHEM & the	
Sof CHAPELLE	30	2 a.m.	Battalion relieved 10th Bn SOUTH WALES BORDERERS in right WEZ MACQUART (CHAPELLE) Sailly & FLEURIE & L'ARMÉE SWITCHES. A very quiet day. Some 500 shells in early morning afternoon very quiet.	
D'ARMENTIÈRES	31		Orders received for relief of Bn at night by 9th Bn. NORTHUMBERLAND FUSILIERS prior to possible move South.	

H Brown 2nd Lieut for Lieut. Col.
Commanding 2nd/5th King's Own Royal Lancaster R.